How I Became a Jezebel and God Delivered Me

How I Became a Jezebel and God Delivered Me

Shonda Kirk

Order this book online at www.trafford.com
or email orders@trafford.com

Most Trafford titles are also available at major online book retailers.

Printed in the United States of America.

ISBN: 978-1-4669-7047-2 (sc)
ISBN: 978-1-4669-7048-9 (e)

Trafford rev. 12/05/2012

 www.trafford.com

North America & international
toll-free: 1 888 232 4444 (USA & Canada)
phone: 250 383 6864 ♦ fax: 812 355 4082

CONTENTS

WORD OF THANKS

would like to thank the Almighty God, my creator, who gave me the words to this awesome work. I believe and pray this would be a blessing to everyone who readit.

I thank my loving husband, Joe, who always asks me before I was complete with writing this book, "Are you done yet?" Also to my three children, Cieara, Jeremiah, and Joshua, you are my inspiration and motivation in the success God will do through this book.

Last but not least, I thank God for my grandmother Robena, who inspires me always that I can do anything I want to do. Also to my pastors, Richard and Clara Brown III, you are one-in-a-million pastors. I am so proud to call you my spiritual parents. You intrigue me to do more and more to leave a legacy for this generation.

"Think big in small places."

INTRODUCTION

This book introduces Christians who can be manipulative, controlling, and Jezebels to establish their way. Although this is not a popular subject, it is one that has to have a resolution.

I have written this book as a way to give men and women a way out of bondage. *How I Became a Jezebel and the Lord Delivered Me* is for people who don't know what to do in situations. Also it shares information to help families that are faced with problems that cannot be resolved within the home.

I pray it changes lives as the book is held in the hands of who will read and grasp this information, and I pray it becomes a *rhema* word to them. I pray God will minister, deliver, transform, and renew your mind from the old way of thinking to the destiny God has ordained for your life.

May this book be a blessing to your life in the wonderful name of Jesus!

Amen.

Shonda Kirk

INDEPENDENCE
VERSUS HUMILITY

an making sure your home is kept together be a hard-core independence later in life? When it comes to holding your family together, most women take the role of who was before them.

Are some marriages torn and divorced because of women who don't quite know what it is to stand back and allow their husband to take leadership?

I share with you a life of seeing women cook, clean, take care of children, work, mow the lawn, lead in the church, and continually want the man's leadership without breaking boundaries.

God has made men interesting creatures of new creations of Him who focuses on one thing at a time. For example, my husband, Joe, is such a loving husband. He is the humblest guy I know! After retiring from the United States Marine Corps, he took on the task of taking care of our three children, Cieara, Joshua, and Jeremiah. I was called to start our new business in childcare and could not be at our home as I desired. My husband's desire was to make sure he took care of our family physically, so he took on the task of all the house responsibility—cooking, washing clothes, cleaning the house, taking our children to school, sport practices, helping children wit homework, etc. As time passed, he began to share with me how his life was becoming after taking care of the home after retiring from the United States Marine Corps. He let me know it was not easy, but he learned a lesson about being at home as a man. My husband said, "Babe, how you do this?" I was like, "What?" He shared, "I can only do one thing at a time, but I learned you are a multitasker and I can only think one thing and do one thing at a time because that is the way God made me." I was like, "Wow. So that is why you could not finish what we needed to accomplish as a family on the day you started." As a wife and a woman of God, I saw for myself the way God has called women and men, and it is not the same calling.

I share with you, ladies, no one will ever do a job like you, but allow your husband to do the job their way. I had to receive a revelation on this day, and it was not who did the job at home as how they did it but that it was done. Our husbands do not fold clothes, cook, clean, take care of the house like we do, but they do it, and that is all that matters.

For example, the first few years of my marriage were a mess. My husband was so humble in his character, but I knew he was getting tired of me. I was independent and wanted things my way or no way. I hated to hear opinions from him and wanted only what I wanted. "I, I, I" was all it was in my first few years of marriage. It made me feel good to be in control. It was like a drive for independence. Maybe it was just like a scar of hurt getting my way. God was speaking to me as He always did, that I was wrong, but in all things I felt it was right. Regardless of how I felt, the word of God says in 2 Corinthians 5:7 that we are to walk by faith and not by sight. As much as I know that, it felt so good and satisfying. Each time I would go in God's presence, He reminded me of my selfishness. The selfishness leads to lashing out and uncontrollable mind-set of wild thoughts.

As time went on, it was as if I came to a standstill in my life. I was just evolving in life, and God was not allowing me to go forward. I often think of it now and thank God. James 4:6 says, "Submit yourselves therefore to God. Resist the devil, and he will flee" (King James Version). It was a fight after being the one in charge, and trying to give God everything required a low and meek heart. So each time I would get in God's presence, He would deal with me and then give me a test with people. Yes, with people. Did I fail? Yes. Did it hurt me? Yes. God wants to take us from independence to humility. When John the Baptist prayed, he said he wanted God to increase, but he decrease. Do you want God to empower you to increase spiritually in Him? I am not ashamed to share with you who are reading this book now that the almighty God has put me in this situation to humble me. God loves you, and He has you in a place in Him that will cause you to only depend on Him and not yourself. Humility is a condition of the heart. We believers must choose to shift from independence to humility.

CHARACTERISTICS OF INDEPENDENCE VERSUS HUMILITY

INDEPENDENCE   HUMILITY

INDEPENDENCE	HUMILITY
SELFWILL	GENTLENESS
REBELLION	KINDNESS
FALSE HUMILITY	SUBMISSION
STUBBORNNESS/PRIDE	PREFERENCE OF OTHERS BEFORE ONESELF
DISOBEDIENCE	OBEDIENCE
HATRED	LOVE OF CHRIST

The chart on the previous page provides only a few descriptions of how we can be used in our flesh and not be aware. Allowing God to minister to us about our life errors helps us depend on God and not ourselves. Sometimes it is so surprising how God tries to get our attention by using natural things and people. I recall many times when God would use the humblest man in the world, my husband, Joe. He is not a man of anger but just likes everything to go smooth. His character of Christ was used in the early years of our marriage. Seeing him live a life and character of Christ while I acted like a pretty fool was amazing. God has a purpose and a plan, and it's not independence; it is having a humble heart.

Jesus said, "Whoever shall exalt himself shall be abased, and he that shall humble himself shall be exalted" (Matthew 23:14).

Humility is powerful. Humility does not mean you are weak, but you are willing to have someone be a leader, and you follow. Humility can be defined as doing something you don't want to do because you desire to show a character of Christ. We will take a look at independence and humility versus one another in the next chapter.

HUMILITY VERSUS INDEPENDENCE

 umility is a choice. A choice of self-control and not wanting to always want what you want.

As a director of childcare services, I have learned to prefer my employees more than myself. I believe Precious Ones Tender Care would not be as successful as it is if it were for individuals who show the love of Christ to one another. God uses people to humble you in situations He allows us in. It is very painful when God gives you the same test over and over, and it seems that you will never pass. God requires us to obey His word and walk in it the best we can. Prayer and fasting helps kill the fleshly motives associated with humility and independence. As believers, we have to sacrifice our own self-will to what God wants to do.

In a group setting, humility is so needed. The main reason people cannot be humble is because of independence or pride. I remember several occasions when I was right, but not humble. I was wrong, but not humble. When humility is being displayed, there is an attitude that follows. So many Christians have a stuck-out chest and proud look that can only be used in pride or the spirit of the Leviathan. The Bible says in Job 41: 15 His scales are his pride, shut up together as with a close seal. Independence is the same way; it takes a person time to live a humble life in Christ, depending on how long the person wants to take. Independence is the same way; it has to be broken, uprooted, and cast off a person. We know it does not take God a long time to do anything. Sometimes, in our Christian life, we hold up the process; it has nothing to do with God. The book of 1 st John 1: 9 says, if we confess our faults one to another, God will forgive us and cleanse us from all unrighteousness. When God does something, He does it as soon as we decide to humble ourselves. In the book of Proverbs, it states God resists the proud, but gives grace to the humble. Oh my, we have a lot of work to do when it comes to humility. Please understand that humility is a lifestyle, not something we put on and take off. Pride is the one thing that will keep us out of fellowship with God. A person has to choose to walk in humility and not allow the spirit of pride to come back to make residency. God honors humility. Anything God honors is good. Humility kills pride. If you are a prideful person, you always think you know everything. Repentance is the first step to please God. What God does not honor, Satan uses to cause division. Satan loves division. Independence is not God's purpose. There is a natural independence of oneself that God has given every person, but when it is used in an authoritative way, it is not led by God, but man. Pride is sin. When we put anything before God—our jobs, money, family, pastors, homes, etc.—that is not humility. Humility is love. Humility is strength. Humility is power. Power to know God can and will help us if we help ourselves.

I often face this in my marriage. Although I have been married several years, I still face the womanhood of my earlier days of being single. I have learned it's not my way, but God's way. The days are over when believers think that when they give their life to Christ, everything is going to fall in place. Yes, by faith it does, but when the test of life comes, we will need to work the Word so the Word will get in our hearts so we might not sin against God, as Psalms 119:11 states.

When I first got married, I would always make it a big deal where we would have a date. It was to the point where God revealed himself to me through my husband. It took my husband prayers and a quiet spirit to humble me to be the woman I am today, to better be a helpmate to him (Genesis 2:15). Ladies, you desire to have peace in your home. Do you want God to move in your behalf in areas you never dreamed of? Humility is the key to a marriage that is destined for greatness. Learning to yield our thoughts, opinions, and decisions for one another—that is humility. God's ultimate goal in marriage is that two people become one. Unity brings forth many things that God will use to mature a relationship between a man and a woman. Humility is a choice we must make in every situation.

Humility versus independence is a no-win streak; it takes you to a place in God you have never known.

Humility is a choice: each day we must make a choice to humble ourselves in every situation.

HUMILITY FACES
A FIGHT

aul stated, "When I try to do right, evil is always present." The fight is within us. James 4:1 says, "Whence come wars and whence come fighting among you? Come they not hence even of your pleasures that war in your members?" Are all the problems in the world faced with selfishness of oneself? Is the world a place that pushes everyone down in a crab pot and not push the kingdom of God or another man's agenda? The Bible says, "God resisted the proud but gives grace to the humble" (James 4:6). There will always be a war in our flesh if we allow ourselves to be governed by our flesh.

The greatest fight I have seen for humility is when a person desires their own way and not the will of God. The Word of God is God's will, and that settles it. It is not about what we think. God never said there would not be challenges or obstacles in life. The challenge is our character being changed and our minds being renewed.

I recall a story of a preacher who began to minister about powerless believers. He began to share how we as Americans have all the nice things, such as cars, houses, clothes, etc.; but we cannot control ourselves nor do we trust God's Holy Spirit to empower us to be able to humble ourselves in the most difficult situations with an individual or people.

Remember each time we choose to humble ourselves, we win a test with God. The good thing about God is, He does not flunk His children; He always gives us a chance to make an A. Choose humility instead of the war that is within you, and let the light of God shine bright.

WHAT IS GOD
REQUIRING OF ME?

an we agree God is requiring something from us as His children? What is God requiring? Let's look at first James 4:7: "Submit you to God." *Submit* is a word that seems like poison to the mere woman or man in marriage, but the Bible is so clear in saying "submit to Him." *Submission* means choosing to do something regardless of how you feel and whether you desire to do it or not. Submission is only done through perfect love, agape (unconditional love). Submission has always been hard because I saw the person's faults, and I could not understand why I needed to submit to a person when they have done me wrong. I will admit I have failed many tests with God because of this kind of stinky thinking. God has ministered many times about what He is requiring of me. Oh boy! I cry, cry, and cry, saying, "Lord, did you see what they did? Father, did you see what they said? Father, I did nothing." Then of course, I would have my self-pity party, wanting someone to come to my rescue and say I was right.

Sometimes when we are in our pity party, it seems we only hear God when we want to hear Him. When it comes to submitting, we think God does not see the other person. But only when we allow God to change us does He will move on our behalf. Of course, we know God is not a respecter of persons (Acts 10:34). God wants to give every person a life that is focused on Him as being their priority.

Ultimately, I had to choose to submit. The choice was mine to keep my mouth closed and privately ask God for insight. I had to choose to endure as a good soldier when I was done wrong by my family, church, and business.

God fulfills His Word when we submit to Him (James 4:7-8). God says He will draw nigh to us when we draw nigh to Him. What an awesome thing it is to allow God to do the work when we obey what He has commanded us to do. We realize the reward of submission is receiving the best from God.

God is requiring submission in these hours
more than ever before.

WHEN I GIVE IN
AND GIVE UP

The part about giving up when the spirit of pride comes is letting you release yourself. When self is released, God opens the door to come in. James 4:6 says, "God resisted the proud but gives grace to the humble." When we submit ourselves to God, He is obligated to come to our rescue as a father would to a child that chooses to make a great choice. I am reminded of when I was growing up as a teenager, and I refused to listen to my grandmother a lot of times because I wanted to hang out late, not come home, and be a wild child. As I think about it now and I am raising my own children, I was the worst child in the world. I would break all kinds of curfews when I was told what time to be home. Yes, my grandmother would ground me, but she always showed me the God-kind of love only a true believer of Christ could give. I was rebellious, stubborn, and so disagreeable about most of the guidelines she would set at our home. She never stopped feeding, clothing, or taking me shopping. When we do not follow through on our Bible contract God has set for us, He still loves us with an unconditional love only He can give to us.

Giving in and *giving up* means we surrender all. When we surrender, the true love of Christ is revealed. Sometimes people think He is going to do everything for them and they are not required to do anything. If God says "Humble yourself," He is asking us to create an atmosphere of His Word on the earth. We are God's children, and He wants us to constantly yield to Him.

One thing I have discovered by giving in and giving up
is the love of Jesus He shares with me and His people.

GOD RELEASES HIS POWER TO UPBUILD ME

fter giving in and giving up, a person sometimes finds himself in a place of loneliness. It's almost like God has left you the minute you choose to allow Him to come in to the places in your heart only He can make whole. The joy of giving in and giving up is that it feels as if you can only trust God, as Proverbs 3:5 states, "Trust in the Lord with all your heart and lean not unto your own understanding." We have to give God our fear, anxiety, hurts, weights, etc. God has to come to our aid as a Band-Aid. You know what a natural Band-Aid does; it covers the scar. The scar is still there, but the Band-Aid covers what is hurting and protects it from continually getting injured. As we look at this analogy, this is how the Lord God is our spiritual Band-Aid. He covers, protects, and heals us, but it's not for days or weeks like the natural Band-Aid. His touch heals us automatically. When God heals us, unlike the Band-Aid, it's then. God is a "now" god! Our mind, heart, soul, spirit, and body are healed the moment we trust in God. Everything is made whole and new. God is a god that gives us the power to stand when we may be going through a major battle. God releases His power, His dynamite, and His dynamic strength to endure. Unlike the Band-Aid, God heals every area when the Band-Aid can only heal one area at a time. Also when a Band-Aid is taken off before the scar is healed or the due time, the wound does not heal properly. When we choose to take our covering of Christ off before time, we allow ourselves to be caught off guard. Believers must constantly keep their armor of God spoken in. Ephesians 6:10-13 says to take up the armor of God. God will always release His power to build us up when we decide to humble ourselves by giving in and giving up. The power of God is what is released at the time to meet a need you may have then. For example, if I were a prideful person and want things my way all the time,

God's power for me at the time is giving in and giving up first and allowing myself to be quiet before the Lord. Quietness is powerful! Sometimes when we speak things and it's not the right timing, place, or season, God will and cannot change His plan for a plan we may have or want that does not follow His Word. God is not a fly-by-night god. He is the same today, yesterday, and forevermore (Hebrews 13:8).

I remember when God spoke to my husband, Joe, to retire in Okinawa, Japan. You know I was not feeling it! I wanted to be with my family. God was doing miracles in Wilson, North Carolina, just like in Okinawa, Japan. I had to choose to say, "Okay, baby, I am going to trust the God in you," and we retired in Okinawa, Japan. I did not immediately humble myself at first; maybe that is why the military headquarters wanted to move us to several duty stations before retirement. Maybe I was the one that was opening that door up because of my thinking. Family ties sometimes cause more problems in a marriage than you can ever imagine. I had to leave and cleave. God came to me with a revelation from my husband in the year of 2010, and it was to stay in Okinawa, Japan. We are currently in a life-changing ministry, entrepreneurs, and enjoying the Lord with our three children. God always has a way of giving His power to us no matter what the storms are. Yes, there will be thunder that roars, lighting that strikes, and rain that falls, but overall, the power of God causes His son Jesus to shine in every situation.

Allow God's power to be released when
you give in and give up.

THE HEALING
PROCESS

As anything in life that needs a healing process, so do our hearts. Our hearts undergo circumcision when we give up and give in the process of God or His Word. We must remember, it's not an overnight process to yield daily. Paul says, "If I find then the law that I would do good, evil is present." Paul continues to say who shall save us: "He thank God through Jesus Christ our Lord will save us."

The wonderful thing about the healing process is, God loves to heal His people. The Lord says healing is for His people

(Isaiah 58:8, that "healing shall spring forth speedily.") Healing is available by God when healing needs to take place. God wants His people healed through every situation they may face. When it comes to being from the spirit of Jezebel, it's the same. The spirit of Jezebel controls you and the people that you are involved with. Sometimes people are being manipulated, and they do not know it, whether it's in relationships on a work force, business, church, marriage, or any relationship where one person is always in control. A lot of women are groomed in a house where there is no male figure or the woman has a male figure and he allows the woman to dominate him. I will give you an example: when a man is not able to think on his own and always has to get his wife to make a decision for him, that is not good. A man was made to be the head (Ephesians 5:23); a wife was given to the man to be a helpmate. I like to say "Help the man meet the things that God has called for his life and their life together." I have been in this situation. I started to notice these ways and how my husband, Joe, would react when I would not allow him to make a decision. Whether the decision at the end was worse or not, still, allowing him not to make the decisions in our first few years of marriage made our marriage a living hell. I am not saying, ladies, you don't have a right to say anything in your marriage, but God loves agreement. Amos 3:3 says, "How can two walk together except they agree." Sometimes we need to go before God as a wife and ask God what it is. "What is the problem my husband and I have?" I asked God, and He said, "You have taken on the ways of the people before you when you were younger." So as I grew in the Lord, He began to show me this ugly picture of how I became a Jezebel through the woman that was before me who taught me in my home, church, and jobs.

The best way to be free from the Jezebel spirit—or any other spirit, I believe—is to do the opposite of what it wants you to do and do what God wants you to do. The spirit of Jezebel loves being in control of everything. The spirit can be used in a man or woman. We know in the Bible that the spirit was used in a woman to control a king and a kingdom (1 Kings 19:5). Pride is the strongest spirit associated in the spirit of Jezebel because this spirit is very stiff, naked, and bigheaded. It takes fasting and prayer to break this spirit as any other spirit of Satan.

I can proudly say that God has delivered me only because I have chosen to be delivered and stay delivered. I face times when I can be used by Satan, but I chose to be used by God, for He is my father. I take joy in knowing that God loved me when I was not being obedient. Obedience reaps very fruitful benefits. The Bible says, "We eat the fruit of the land" (Isaiah 1:19).

As we humble ourselves when we identify our wrongs, it opens the door for God to come in and Satan and flesh to leave out. God cannot use an unclean vessel. 1 Corinthians 6:19 says, "Do we not know that our temple or body is the Holy Spirit which is in you, which ye have from God and ye are not your own." Some people say they are in control of their own body, and they can do what they want. When you are a believer of Jesus you have to obligate yourself to Him totally. Also people often say they love God but do not give God everything. In our healing process, instead of rebelling or bucking. Why? I often say the problem is never with God; it's with us. In order for us to receive God's healing, we must commit to humility in every area of our lives, but most of all, we must trust God to heal us. I love what the Bible says in Matthew 11:28: "Come unto me all who are weary and heavy-laden, and I will give you rest. Take my yoke upon you and learn of me, for I am gentle and humble in heart and you will find rest for your souls, for my yoke is easy, and my burden is light." Wow! God says if we make the first move, He will take all our baggage, and He will make exchange for us. It's like living in Okinawa, Japan, and our family received US dollars for work done. We go to an exchange to receive Japanese yen for what we need to purchase. When we receive yen, we have made an exchange for what we need at that time. God is the same way. When healing is needed, God says, "Bring all your hurts, disappointment, trials, tribulation, etc., to me, and I will give you what you desire . . . Rest for your souls." God guarantees that we will have rest. Although the Japanese yen rate may change, God's exchange never changes; it is the same any time of any day. The healing process is always surrounded by God being available to help us through any dilemma.

The truth is, before we are healed, we are healed according to the word in Matthew 8:17. Jesus took every hurt, offense, abuse, lie, etc.; everything is nailed to the cross. No more shall we desire to remain in pain, sickness, shame, and disappointments. Isaiah 53:5 clearly states, "By His stripes we are healed." Live out your healing today.

CHOOSING TO
STAY HEALED

ave you been healed of something and you feel like after receiving your healing, you are not healed? Well, that's a lie from the devil. Can I release into you a truth? *You are, you were, you have been healed!* No second thinking! Either God is lying or you. Who? We know the Word of God says, in Numbers chapter 23 verse 19, "God is not a man that He should lie, nor the son of man, that He should repent." Has He said something and not done it? Or has He spoken and not make it good?

The only problem in choosing to stay healed is when a person has a mind of doubt. Believers please God with our faith, and He rewards us according to Hebrews 11:6.

God is not after how we feel.
He wants us to speak of healing.

verall, I believe this book is an eye-opener to the spirit of Jezebel. It shares very detailed information to help any person who desires to be delivered from the spirit of Jezebel. As believers, we should never think we have everything in our lives in order. We are a work in progress. This is the reason we gave our lives to God—for us to receive help from Him to better our lives. I want to reassure you, you are a child of God, but sometimes when we receive salvation, we think everything gets saved. Our spirit is saved, but our character has a lot of junk God wants to purge out to be an effective witness for Christ. When we submit to God, He always gives us more than what we ask Him for. Do not allow the spirit of Jezebel to be used in your desire to be led by the spirit of God.

May God add a blessing to you after you have read this book.

Mrs. Shonda Kirk

Printed in the United States
By Bookmasters